Presented to

**Clear Lake City - County Freeman
Branch Library**

By

Friends of the Freeman Library

THE
STORY
of THE
HOOVER DAM

A HISTORY PERSPECTIVES BOOK

Kelly Milner Halls

Published in the United States of America by Cherry Lake Publishing
Ann Arbor, Michigan
www.cherrylakepublishing.com

Consultants: J. David Rogers, PhD, PE, PG, and Karl F. Hasselmann Chair in Geological
Engineering, Missouri University of Science & Technology; Marla Conn, ReadAbility, Inc.
Editorial direction: Red Line Editorial
Book design and illustration: Sleeping Bear Press

Photo Credits: AP Images, cover (left), 1 (left), 7, 10, 12, 14, 17, 23, 27, 30; U.S. Bureau of
Reclamation/Library of Congress, cover (middle), 1 (middle), 20, 21; Harris & Ewing/
Library of Congress, cover (right), 1 (right); Ben Shahn/Library of Congress, 4; North
Wind/North Wind Picture Archives, 5

Library of Congress Cataloging-in-Publication Data

Halls, Kelly Milner, 1957-
  The story of the Hoover Dam / Kelly Milner Halls.
    pages cm. -- (Perspectives library)
  Includes bibliographical references.
  ISBN 978-1-62431-668-5 (hardcover) -- ISBN 978-1-62431-695-1 (paperback)
-- ISBN 978-1-62431-722-4 (PDF) -- ISBN 978-1-62431-749-1 (hosted ebook)
  1. Hoover Dam (Ariz. and Nev.)--History--Juvenile literature. 2. Dams--Colorado River
(Colo.-Mexico)--History--Juvenile literature. 3. Dams--Colorado River (Colo.-Mexico)--
Design and construction--Juvenile literature. 4. Construction workers--Colorado River
(Colo.-Mexico)--History--Juvenile literature. I. Title.

  TC557.5.H6H35 2014
  627'.820979313--dc23
                              2013029717

Cherry Lake Publishing would like to acknowledge the work of
The Partnership for 21st Century Skills. Please visit *www.p21.org*
for more information.

Printed in the United States of America
Corporate Graphics Inc.
January 2014

TABLE OF CONTENTS

In this book, you will read about the story of the Hoover Dam from three perspectives. Each perspective is based on real things that happened to real people who were involved in or experienced the building of the Hoover Dam. As you'll see, the same event can look different depending on one's point of view.

Stuart Latimer

River Explorer

I'm quite old now, just over 70, but when I was a boy of nine, an orphan with no one and nothing, I tagged along on a great adventure with John Wesley Powell. Powell was a Union major in the Civil War, but he had a love for adventure and exploration. In 1869, he set out to map the Colorado River's path for 900 miles, including the winding stretch that passes through the Grand Canyon. Powell hired nine men to help him, and I tagged along in secret.

The group started out in Wyoming Territory. I hid in a storage locker and wasn't discovered until Utah, and by then it was too late to send me back. For weeks we rode down the river, experiencing trial after trial. Boats were lost and crushed against the rapids. One man left the expedition because the journey was so difficult. Once we came to the Grand Canyon in August, the waters were as wicked as the walls were high. Three more men abandoned the party within the Grand Canyon and were never seen again.

....

John Wesley Powell and his team faced dangerous rapids while exploring the Colorado River. ▶

We finally made it out of the Grand Canyon bruised and hungry, but alive. Powell was able to map the river, but he was forever cautious about taming it. He believed in using dams on the river to provide much-needed **irrigation** for farmland, but only after the Southwest had been more carefully studied.

Those wanting a dam built on the Colorado River did not share Powell's concern. So they picked another explorer's report to base their decision on. Joseph Christmas Ives had explored the Colorado River 12 years before Powell, in 1857. After an equally perilous journey, moving upstream as far as Black Canyon, he concluded that it would be a good place for a dam.

It wasn't until December 1928 that President Calvin Coolidge finally signed the Boulder Canyon

SECOND SOURCE

▶ Find another source that describes Ives's Colorado River exploration. Compare the information there to the information in this chapter.

Project Act. This gave the okay for building the dam. Then it took Congress two and a half more years to authorize the $165 million needed for the project. It's 1931 now, and construction is starting this year on the massive dam.

▲ *Black Canyon in the Colorado River was chosen for the dam site.*

THINK ABOUT IT

▶ Determine the main idea of this paragraph. Provide one piece of evidence that supports it.

People have wanted to build a dam in this area of the Colorado River for many years. The American Southwest is a desert, and water is precious. Farming in much of the region is usually not an option because there is not enough water for crops. But the Boulder Dam will change all this. The redirected flow of the Colorado River will provide water for irrigation so farmers can plant crops in the Palo Verde, Imperial, and Coachella Valleys downstream.

It's not just the water that will spur the transformation. It is also the mud. The same **silt** that turns the river as red as an Arizona sunset turns rocky soil into **fertile** farmland. Just ask the tribal elders of the Ute, the Mohave, the Hopi, and the Navajo. For generations, those tribes have known the riches of farming the natural floodplains of the Colorado River.

Once water is available in the desert, wanderers are transformed into farmers, and cities spring up around them. Just look at the Imperial Valley in southeastern California. The Alamo Canal was dug to redirect a portion of the Colorado River to the desert valley, and it became a virtual oasis. People were able to farm, and their crops blossomed. Life was great until the Colorado River swelled with the **runoff** from the Colorado Rockies. The swollen river overwhelmed the small canal floodgates. Over the next two years, crops and farmlands were flooded by several feet of water and the Salton Sea was formed. The dam and new distribution canals were needed to protect the farms from the damage of future floods.

Another reason for the dam is to provide **hydroelectric** power to the region. This will pay for the construction of the dam over the next 50 years. The power and volume of the river will allow a lot

▲ *A crowd gathered in 1930 to celebrate the start of the Boulder Dam project.*

of electricity to be produced. This electricity will be a huge resource to people in the region.

But the Colorado River will not be easily tamed. Most of us who have traveled the river know it.

The river is dangerous and has taken too many Americans. Some parts are slow and steady, but others slam into jagged boulders or drop like an elevator. The river can turn tree trunks into splinters. I've been exploring the river all my life, and I know this all too well.

HYDROELECTRIC POWER

The power plant at the Hoover Dam diverts water through 17 main turbines to generate electricity. Each year, the Hoover Dam creates an average of 4.2 billion kilowatt-hours of electricity. This allows the plant to provide Arizona, California, and Nevada with some of their electricity.

Sara Meyer

Daughter of a Dam Worker

Grammy cried the day we left Canton, Ohio, on April 18, 1931. She told my mama it was going to be tough and held my hand so tight it brought tears to my eyes. Mama cried too, but she said she had no choice. Papa was going. He was off to build that big dam, the one we had read about in the paper, and we had to stay together. So off we went—Mama, Papa, my little brother, Scotty, and me. We had all the belongings we were taking with us in the back of our truck.

Times had been hard for our family. Papa had run out of odd jobs to do in Grammy's town. We moved in with her after Papa lost his job once the **Great Depression** got underway. We could barely afford food anymore. I knew my family and those in our small town were having difficulties making ends meet. But I overheard my parents saying thousands of others across the country had been knocked off their feet as well. It seems the Great Depression is making it hard for people all over to find work.

We were lucky, Papa said. We had a little money left, but it was running out quickly. Thousands of folks were out of money already. Thousands of kids

THINK ABOUT IT

▶ Determine the main idea of this paragraph. Provide one piece of evidence that supports it.

▲ *A group of jobless and homeless people stood in line to apply for jobs during the Great Depression.*

were hungry because of it. But there was work in Nevada. Heading there was our chance to keep food in our bellies. So I said good-bye to my friends and headed west with my family.

Days passed and the sun was going down before we got to that rocky nowhere Papa called our new home. "Welcome to Ragtown," a sign said in hand-painted letters. It sure wasn't Canton. To start, there wasn't a single building in sight. Folks were living in tents or huts made of blankets. Many lived out of and slept in their cars.

We drove our truck to a place on the edge of the group of people. As we passed by, I noticed how the grown-ups looked tired and worn-out. The kids looked dirty, like they hadn't had a bath in a long time. Once we made camp, I had to go to the bathroom. Mama asked a stranger where the bathrooms were. She laughed and said just about any hole would do in a pinch. There wasn't a toilet for more than 30 miles.

It was hard to fall asleep that night in our truck bed, but it was harder to sleep in the morning. The minute the sun came up it got blisteringly hot. There were no trees nearby that could offer us shade. Papa walked to the edge of the camp, where applications and hiring were handled. Mama seemed to hold her breath until he got home. She told Scotty and me to collect sticks for firewood. The one with the most sticks would get a jelly bean. Someone nearby overheard our conversation. She told us to watch out for rattlesnakes and scorpions. They were pretty common where we were.

I was scared, and my face showed it. So the lady asked her son Irby to tag along with us. I was happy to have the help. As we walked, he showed us where most folks went to the bathroom and where scrap twigs were easier to find.

ANALYZE THIS

▶ Analyze the accounts of Stuart Latimer and Sara Meyer. How are they different? How are they similar?

▲ *Dam workers spent long hours in the hot desert sun.*

When I asked him if he had any brothers or sisters, a tear came to his eye. He said he used to have a baby sister, but she was gone now. She couldn't take the heat last summer. When it hit 130 degrees, she fussed a little and then fell asleep. She never woke up. We didn't say a word the whole walk home. I gathered the most wood, so I got the jelly bean. But I gave it to Irby. I didn't know what else to do.

By the time Papa got home, we'd built a shelter just like the one next door, except our quilts were cleaner. Mama even swept all the stones off our dirt floor so eating our can of beans was like a picnic. Papa's hands were red and swollen. He said he had landed a job for $2.25 per day. He was working on the top level of the drilling jumbo. This was a mobile platform four stories tall. Papa and the others on the drilling jumbo used **jackhammers** to break up the rock in the walls of Black Canyon.

Mama was worried about him doing such dangerous work. But she was relieved he had gotten a job so we would be able to afford food for our family.

THE FINISHED DAM

Construction of the dam took four years. The dam was completed in 1935, two and a half years ahead of schedule. Originally known as the Boulder Dam, the structure was renamed the Hoover Dam in 1947. It is 726 feet tall at its highest point and 1,244 wide feet at its widest point. The dam is 660 feet thick at its base and only 45 feet thick at the top. It was the largest and highest concrete dam in the world when it was completed.

3

Butch Wilson

High Scaler

As a kid, I thought my destiny was set. I thought I would walk the high wire and swing from the trapeze, like my parents did. Being the star of the circus was what I was born to be. But in my teens, things changed.

The Great Depression came upon us, and folks couldn't afford to go to the circus anymore. Without an audience, we didn't get paid.

If I wanted to work, I figured I'd have to leave New York for Black Canyon on the Colorado River in Nevada, where folks were building a giant dam.

The newspaper said a group of construction companies called Six Companies was hiring 7,000 workers to build the dam. Rumor was that more than 12,000 people had applied. I hopped a freight train for Las Vegas, Nevada, the closest town to the canyon. From Las Vegas, I hitched a ride to the workers' camp, 30 miles east. Whole families were living there, right in the middle of a desert. Some slept in tents. Some slept in

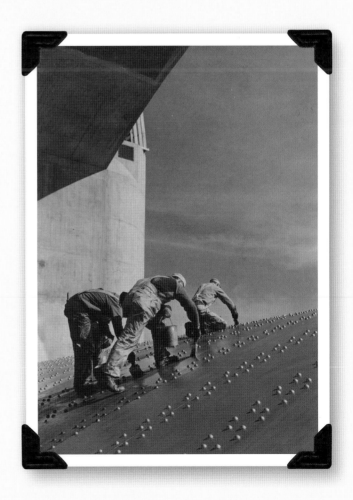

Workers had to be careful, as construction accidents were common. ▶

their cars—or under them, when it was too hot to sleep inside. Little kids were filthy, but so were their parents.

As I walked through the camp, a man asked if I was hoping to get work, and I said yes. His name was Skip, and he told me to bunk near his tent. The next morning, he would show me where to catch the bus that would take us to the dam site. He said he'd introduce me to his foreman and point out Frank Crowe. He was the superintendent of construction of the dam, so he was the guy running the show.

Once I told Skip's foreman what I had done back in New York, a smile crossed his face and he said two words: "high scaler." It was the best-paying job at the dam. I'd take home $3.50 per day. A lot of other guys received around $2 per day. But when I said that sounded great to me, all the color drained out of Skip's face.

It turned out that high scalers got paid more for a reason. As a high scaler, I would sit on a

boatswain's chair, which is basically a small bench
with a harness. Then I would be lowered from the
canyon walls on ropes until I was 500, 600, or even
700 feet above the canyon floor. I would use a
jackhammer to drill blast holes that dynamite

▲ *Workers put the finishing touches on the dam 700 feet above the*
Colorado River.

would be stuck in. Once the dynamite exploded, I would use a jackhammer again to knock the loose rock off the canyon walls.

Most folks said no thank you to this type of risky work when they saw how high the canyon was. But I'm not most folks. This was just my type of crazy. I had found my new destiny: I was made to help build this dam.

My first day on the job was August 15, 1931. I was shown how to pound steel fasteners into the top of the canyon wall to secure my ropes— one for my boatswain's chair, one for my safety belt, and one for my jackhammer. Then I practiced **rappelling** down the rocky face of the canyon with the rope in my hands and my feet against the stone.

SECOND SOURCE

▶ Find a second source about the work high scalers did on the dam. How does the information compare to what you read in this chapter?

On my second day, an explosion close by nearly knocked me off my chair. I was told that it would be loud, but I wasn't prepared for how loud and powerful the blast was. The explosion sound seemed to ricochet off the canyon walls and double in volume. There was a horrible ringing in my ears after that, continuing with each new explosion. I could hardly hear while I was up on the canyon wall.

In fact, I didn't hear the warning cries the day Jack Russell died on September 21, 1931. He was the first high scaler to die while working on the dam. A big chunk of granite fell from above and nearly hit my right shoulder, but I dodged it.

Jack wasn't so lucky. A sharp edge of the stone hit Jack's head and knocked him off his chair. His safety belt must not have been attached properly, because I watched him fall the 400 feet to the bottom of the canyon. It was horrible, and I promised myself then that I would always triple-check my harness and ropes.

DAM WORKERS

Thousands of men worked on the construction of the dam throughout the four years it was being built. This included surveyors of the dam site, engineers, and laborers. Officially, 96 people died during construction of the dam. But this does not include the workers who died from carbon monoxide poisoning and heat exhaustion.

The job is risky, but I love it. I see everything from these heights. I see guys on the ground finishing the diversion tunnels. These are four man-made, concrete-lined tunnels intended to carry the Colorado River around the work site while the dam is being constructed. I have seen guys collapse after working

▲ *Once completed, the dam provided irrigation water for farms downstream.*

for hours in 130-degree heat with no shade. The medics then rush them into tubs of ice water to try to revive them.

We high scalers are the movie stars of dam building. People drive out to watch us work, so once in a while, we put on a show. We make sure the boss isn't watching, and then two of us push off from the canyon walls and soar like graceful canyon birds. The people love it. Some of the girls even bake us cookies.

At the end of 1931, Six Companies opened the town of Boulder City in Nevada for us, and things got even better. The people in charge recognized how dangerous Ragtown had become. So they built us a city and moved us workers and families into it. Now I get to rent a room in the men's **dormitory** for cheap. Families get to rent new houses, and the kids are finally back in school. We're fed three square meals a day in the company mess hall for cheap too.

I can eat all I want, enough food for three guys, and the mess hall workers don't say a word.

If the Great Depression isn't over when we finish this dam, I think I'll go with the other guys to Washington State. I hear they will be building the Grand Coulee Dam out there, and I hope I'll be able to get a job with the skills I've gained here. Plus, I'll be able to perform death-defying feats for folks in the Pacific Northwest too. I always did want to be a star.

ANALYZE THIS

▶ Analyze the accounts of Butch Wilson and Stuart Latimer. How are their stories alike? How are they different?

LOOK, LOOK AGAIN

Take a close look at this image showing the end stages of the dam construction and answer the following questions:

1. How would a river explorer react to this picture? Why?

2. What would a child of a dam worker think when she or he saw this picture? How would the child's reaction be different from that of the dam worker?

3. How would a dam worker describe this picture? What thoughts would he or she have when looking at this scene?

GLOSSARY

dormitory (DOR-mi-tor-ee) a building with many separate rooms for sleeping

fertile (FUR-tuhl) good for growing crops

Great Depression (GRAYT di-PRESH-uhn) the economic crisis beginning with the stock market crash in 1929 and continuing through the 1930s

hydroelectric (hye-droh-i-LEK-trik) something that uses the power of water to produce electricity

irrigation (ir-uh-GAE-shuhn) the watering of land by artificial means in order to grow crops

jackhammers (JAK-ham-urs) tools using compressed air for drilling through rock or other hard surfaces by repeated pounding actions

rappelling (ruh-PEL-ing) descending a rope under control on the face of a cliff or canyon

runoff (RUHN-awf) the precipitation that reaches rivers and streams

silt (SILT) very small particles of soil that are carried by flowing water

LEARN MORE

Further Reading

Graham, Ian. *You Wouldn't Want to Work on the Hoover Dam!: An Explosive Job You'd Rather Not Do.* New York: Franklin Watts, 2012.

Mann, Elizabeth. *Hoover Dam.* New York: Mikaya, 2001.

Zuehlke, Jeffrey. *The Hoover Dam.* Minneapolis, MN: Lerner Publications, 2010.

Web Sites

History—Hoover Dam
http://www.history.com/topics/hoover-dam
This Web site has more information, including videos, about the Hoover Dam.

Hoover Dam
http://www.usbr.gov/lc/hooverdam/
Visitors to this Web site will find photographs that were taken during the Hoover Dam's construction.

INDEX

ABOUT THE AUTHOR

Kelly Milner Halls has written nearly 30 books, along with hundreds of magazine and newspaper articles. She lives in Spokane, Washington, with two daughters, two dogs, too many cats, and an iguana.